I want to be a Veterinarian

Written by Peter J

This book belongs to

_____

Peter J. always dreamed of writing stories to inspire children to follow their dreams. Although his career originally took him down other paths, Peter eventually succeeded in becoming a children's book author. He hopes his books will encourage young readers to always believe in themselves. When he's not writing, Peter enjoys reading, traveling, and spending time outdoors. He lives in Chicago with his wife and two kids. Peter looks forward to continuing to write uplifting books that share positive messages with children.

Peter J, from Chicago, USA

Lea loves spending time with animals. She has a dog named Cookie, a cat named Whiskers, a hamster named Nibbels, and a fish tank full of pretty fish. When she grows up, Lea wants to take care of animals every day. "I'll be a veterinarian to heal sick animals," says Lea.

Lea tells her parents she wants to be a veterinarian when she grows up. They take her to visit Dr. Martinez, the local veterinarian. At Dr. Martinez's office, Lea gets to see the examination room and tools that vets use. Dr. Martinez explains how he helps sick pets feel better. Lea loves learning about his job.

At the vet clinic, Lea watches Dr. Martinez examine a parrot with a hurt wing. Dr. Marinez gently wraps the wing in a bandage. Lea is fascinated seeing the vet take care of the parrot. Dr. Martinez explains that being a vet requires learning about all types of animals - birds, lizards, dogs, cats, and more! Lea thinks it would be the perfect job for her.

Lea asks Dr. Martinez all about being a veterinarian. What do you have to study? How do you help sick pets? Do you get to play with animals? Dr. Martinez smiles and answers Lea's questions. He says vet school is a lot of hard work but very rewarding. Lea feels more motivated than ever to achieve her dream.

To become a veterinarian, Lea learns she must study science and care for animals. It will take a lot of hard work in school. Lea is determined to make her dream come true. She starts reading animal books and volunteering at a pet shelter to get experience.

Lea decides to gain more experience with animals. She volunteers at the animal refuge on weekends. Lea gets to help feed the horses and groom the bunnies. She learns how the caretakers tend to the ducks, pigs, and goats, too.

In high school, Lea takes science classes to prepare for veterinary school. She learns biology, chemistry, and anatomy. During summer vacation, Lea volunteers with vets to gain experience. She gets to observe check-ups, surgeries and more.

In veterinary school, Lea works very hard. She learns how to diagnose and treat sick animals. Lea practices giving check-ups, shots and medications. She learns about surgeries and X-rays, too. Lea is gaining at the skills to become a great vet.

After many years of hard work, Lea graduates from veterinary school at the top of her class. All her determination has paid off. She opens her own veterinary clinic to care for pets in the community. Dr. Lea puts up her sign and eagerly waits for her first patients.

Now Dr. Lea gets to live her dream helping animals every day. She treats sick pets, performs check-ups, and makes sure all the animals in town are healthy. Lea loves making a difference in the lives of families and their furry companions. Being a veterinarian is the perfect job for her!

Veterinarian Lea helps a pig when its food gets stuck in its throat.

Veterinarian Lea assists a rabbit that is having trouble breathing.

Veterinarian Lea helps a duck's leg feel better after an accident.

Veterinarian Lea treats every animal with kindness and equality, and she finds joy in assisting them.

Peter J wholeheartedly cheers on every child with dreams, urging them to follow their passions, and sincerely hopes that their dreams come true. If you enjoy Peter J's book, we would truly appreciate your feedback in the form of a review and a star rating. Your thoughts and ratings mean a lot, as Peter J is committed to creating even more enjoyable books for your reading delight. Thank you wholeheartedly for your ongoing support.

By the same author: Peter J
Already published:
I want to be an Astronaut
I want to be a Veterinarian
I want to become a Doctor
I want to be an Engineer
I want to be a Pilot
I want to be a Teacher
Coming soon:
I want to be a Singer
I want to a Football Player
I And more...

Made in the USA
Coppell, TX
10 December 2024

42075940R00024